MARKETING
EFFECTIVELY

MOI ALI

A Dorling Kindersley Book

Dorling Kindersley

LONDON, NEW YORK, SYDNEY, DELHI, PARIS
MUNICH & JOHANNESBURG

Managing Editor Adèle Hayward
Senior Art Editor Jamie Hanson

DTP Designer Julian Dams, Amanda Peers
Production Controller Michelle Thomas

Senior Managing Editor Stephanie Jackson
Senior Managing Art Editor Nigel Duffield

Produced for Dorling Kindersley by
Cooling Brown
9–11 High Street, Hampton
Middlesex TW12 2SA

Creative Director Arthur Brown
Senior Editor Amanda Lebentz
Editor Helen Ridge

First American Edition, 2001

00 01 02 03 04 05 10 9 8 7 6 5 4 3 2 1

Published in the United States by
Dorling Kindersley Publishing, Inc.
95 Madison Avenue,
New York, New York 10016

Library of Congress Cataloging-in-Publication Data

Ali, Moi
    Effective marketing / Moi Ali.
        p. cm – (Essential managers)
    "A Dorling Kindersley book."
    Includes index.
    ISBN 0-7894-7148-5 (alk.paper)
    1. Marketing. I. Title. II. Series.

HP5415 .A427 2000
658.8–dc21
                                    00-047419

Reproduced by Colourscan, Singapore
Printed in Hong Kong by Wing King Tong

See our complete catalog at
www.dk.com

CONTENTS

INTRODUCTION

Marketing is an essential business discipline, and its vital contribution to the success of an organization is widely recognized. Successful marketing results in stronger products, happier customers, and bigger profits. Whether the whole marketing function within your business is your responsibility, or whether it is a peripheral activity, Marketing Effectively will show you how to take a strategic approach to the task. Stay on course with helpful hints, advice, and information and evaluate your skills with a self-assessment exercise. Covering basic concepts such as the marketing mix, essential skills including direct mail, and the fundamentals of marketing strategy, this book is an invaluable guide to improving your marketing performance.

Putting Customers First

Marketing is key to the success of any business and must be customer driven in order to be effective. Make customers your prime focus and reap the rewards.

Understanding Marketing

Marketing is often confused with publicity and promotion, but these are just part of the discipline. Understand all the components of marketing, particularly the central role that customers play, and you will be a step closer to business success.

1 Design your whole business around your customers' needs.

2 Gather as much information as possible on the requirements of potential new customers.

Defining Marketing

Effective marketing is often described as "making what you can sell, not selling what you can make." Organizations that sell what they can make are product led: they make the product first, consider customers afterwards, and see marketing simply as a means of persuading customers to buy. The most successful organizations make what they can sell. They are customer led, creating products and services in response to customer need.

TAKING MARKETING SERIOUSLY

Focus on every aspect of marketing, not just on promotion and sales techniques, to persuade customers to buy. By taking the discipline seriously and acknowledging its influence, you will reap all the benefits that effective marketing has to offer: satisfied, loyal customers, a growing customer base, popular and successful products, increased turnover, more recommendations and repeat business, as well as fewer complaints. The end result of all this is bigger profits, which is one of the most powerful reasons for improving marketing performance. You are also far more likely to enjoy overall business success, and be the envy of your competitors.

3 Try to develop an outward-looking approach to marketing, as opposed to an insular one.

FOCUSING ON CUSTOMERS

Research is conducted into customers' wants

Product or service is designed to meet need

Product or service is made public

Customers buy product or service

Product or service meets customers' need

Customers buy product or service again

IDENTIFYING MARKETING COMPANY TYPES

TYPE OF COMPANY	CHARACTERISTICS
FOREFRONTER Consistently anticipates customers' needs and gets its products to market first.	Innovative and proactive. This type of organization truly understands marketing. It invests in research and product development and devises innovative solutions.
FOLLOWER Dislikes taking risks. Prefers to play it safe and see which way the market will go before deciding whether to take any action.	Lacks pioneering spirit. This type of company might attain success, but its attitude will always limit achievement. A more proactive approach would improve marketing success.
FOSSIL Has always conducted business in the same way and sees no reason to change.	Conservative, insular, and complacent. Such organizations need to develop a more outward focus. Activity must be driven by customer need, not company habit and tradition.

ANALYZING THE MARKETING MIX

The marketing mix is a very simple and successful recipe to follow. Blend its key ingredients – product, price, place, and promotion – in the correct proportions, and you will reap the many benefits of effective, strategic marketing.

> **4** Look at each element of the mix and determine their importance.

> **5** Create the right balance between price and quality.

> **6** Concentrate your efforts on the key elements of the mix.

UNDERSTANDING THE MIX

The marketing mix of product, price, place, and promotion is known as the "Four Ps." Marketing involves developing the right product (one that meets customer need); setting the right price (one that delivers a profit and keeps customers happy); getting the product to the right place (where customers can buy it); and promoting it (to encourage customers to buy it). The ingredients of the mix are the same for all organizations, only quantities vary. Where customers are price-conscious, for example, price dominates the mix and setting the right price is vital.

◀ COMPARING
DIFFERENT MIXES
Two hotels can have very different marketing mixes. For a five-star hotel, product (excellent restaurant, health club facilities, and superior rooms) is the principal ingredient of the mix. Guests expect luxury and accept that they must pay a price for it. For a budget hotel, cost is paramount. Its customers want to be able to stay at an affordable price.

FIVE-STAR HOTEL   BUDGET HOTEL

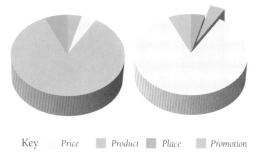

Key   *Price*   *Product*   *Place*   *Promotion*

EXAMINING PROPORTIONS

Devise the right marketing mix, and you will maximize profits. Focus on each element of the mix to determine its importance to your business. Remember that the mix is not static; the perfect proportions today may not produce the desired results next year, or even next week. From time to time you will need to vary the recipe, by reducing prices during quiet periods, for example. There is an interrelationship between the four ingredients of the mix. If a product's price is high, customers will have high expectations. If advertising and promotional activity are significant, these costs will have to be recouped in the price.

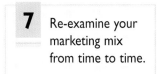

7 Re-examine your marketing mix from time to time.

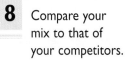

8 Compare your mix to that of your competitors.

CREATING THE RIGHT MARKETING MIX

KEY ELEMENTS

PRODUCT OR SERVICE
Bought by customers to meet a need. The need may be practical (to get rid of stains), emotional (to feel good), or basic (to satisfy hunger).

PRICE
A crucial part of the mix, the price must be right if customers are to buy a product in sufficient quantities to ensure a profit.

PLACE
The "bridge" connecting customers and products, such as a wholesaler, retail outlet, or other distribution system.

PROMOTION
Promotional activity, such as advertising and direct mail, that informs customers what you have to offer and persuades them to buy.

FACTORS TO CONSIDER

● Products and services usually fulfill a number of needs, and it is important to identify which ones your products and services satisify.
● A product or service may satisfy a need that consumers did not even realize they had.

● The right price for quality goods is a fair one. Price and quality must be balanced successfully.
● Fair does not necessarily mean cheap – set the price of a product too low, and customers may assume that its quality is inferior.

● For some niche businesses, place is not an issue – enthusiasts and collectors, for example, are willing to travel long distances to shop.
● The internet provides a new mechanism for bringing customers and company together.

● For most enterprises, promotional activity is essential for attracting customers.
● For businesses that rely on passing trade, promotion is less important, since the right location and products will ensure success.

SETTING THE RIGHT PRICE

Price is the most flexible element of the marketing mix, since you can change it quickly and easily. But your profits depend on getting it right. Selling at low prices means tight profit margins and an overreliance on high sales volume. A downturn in your market can put you out of business. There is no fixed link between price and cost: you can raise prices even if your costs have not increased, and lower them without a cost decrease. Monitor competitors' prices so that you know exactly what is happening in the marketplace, and aim to understand what your competitors' strategies are. Then develop your own pricing strategy. Supply and demand will inevitably affect what you can charge, but aim for a Goldilocks pricing strategy: not too cheap, not too expensive, but just right.

POINTS TO REMEMBER

● Low price is often equated with low quality. Customers might prefer to pay more for an identical product because they are convinced that it is better than a cheaper one.

● Customers do not buy a product simply because it is cheap; they buy because of need. However inexpensive your lawnmowers, you will not sell one to someone without a yard.

● Customers can be less "price aware" than you might expect. Test to see. Find out more about your customers' buying habits and whether they shop around for the best price.

9 Make sure you know what price your competitors are charging.

10 Employ market research to find out how you are perceived by your clients.

SELLING ON VALUE

Consider selling on value rather than price. Price-based sales pitches attract price-sensitive customers who are already in the market for what you are selling. A value-based pitch can woo customers who did not realize they needed your product. For example, a $300 mattress will appeal to customers who are looking for a new mattress at a good price. A mattress guaranteed to ease back pain will open up a new market by appealing to bad back sufferers who were not even considering such a purchase.

QUESTIONS TO ASK YOURSELF

Q What is the value of our offering in terms of saving customers time and effort?

Q Is our offering giving value by enhancing beauty or status?

Q Are we demonstrating that a purchase is not a cost but a good investment?

Q Have we asked what customers most value about our products?

FITTING PR INTO THE MIX

Public relations (PR) is often regarded as the fifth "P" of the marketing mix, standing for perception. A good image is a prerequisite for successful marketing. An attractive product at the right price will not guarantee a sale. Customers do not like to buy from companies with poor reputations. Use PR techniques to enhance your image and shape positive customer perceptions. Consider ways of boosting your image: perhaps your organization could support or sponsor a charity, a worthwhile cause, or local venture, for example. Take the opportunity to build a strong profile by publicizing your achievements in the media.

11 Involve PR staff in marketing decision making.

12 Use research rather than gut feeling to assess customers' needs.

CREATING THE RIGHT IMAGE

Look at the various aspects of your business that customers use to form their view of you. These might include your premises, the telephone manner of staff, and your publicity materials. Examine each of them in detail and work out what kind of image is being conveyed to your customers. Is that the image you want to put across? If not, draw up a plan of action for bringing your desired image into line with your actual image.

◀ **CONVEYING A GOOD IMAGE**
Attractive physical surroundings, committed staff, and well thought-out procedures are all important in conveying a caring and friendly image and giving an organization an edge over its competitors.

Getting to Know Your Customers

Good customer information is key to boosting profit, so it is vital to build up a clear picture of who your customers are. Watch them, talk to them, ask them questions, and find out all that you can in order to give them what they want and keep them happy.

13 Avoid gathering facts for the sake of it; look only for what you can use.

14 Collect information on an ongoing basis by asking new customers a few marketing questions.

Collecting Data

Many organizations have huge customer bases, but it is those who respond to customers' needs to be treated as individuals who are most likely to succeed. By collecting and processing customer data to produce a customer profile and identify customer segments, you can tailor-make products and services for particular groups of key customers. Meet identified customer need and you will sell more products and lose fewer customers. A better understanding of your customers will also enable you to target publicity more accurately.

Profiling Customers

A customer profile provides a picture of your typical customer. Some companies require an in-depth profile, detailing sex, age, income, lifestyle, address and type of housing, number of children, and so on. For others, a simpler profile will suffice. Decide which common characteristics it would be useful to look for in your customers. Business-to-business organizations, for example, may wish to analyze factors such as company size, vehicle fleet size, turnover, and location. Identify the kind of data you need, then plan how to uncover it.

Questions to Ask Yourself

Q What age groups are our customers in, and what is the male/female split?

Q Where do our customers live, and do they travel far to buy?

Q Do they make onetime purchases, or is there an on-going relationship?

Q How much do they spend each month/year?

IDENTIFYING SOURCES OF INFORMATION

SOURCE	FACTORS TO CONSIDER
COMPANY RESOURCES Includes invoices, dispatch notes, mailing lists, and sales statistics.	Existing information can often provide valuable marketing data, such as size of purchase, date of last purchase, and geographic location of customers.
CUSTOMER INTERACTION Includes face-to-face surveys and focus groups.	A good way of eliciting qualitative information about your customers' motivations. Explain that their insights will help you to develop products and services to meet their needs.
CUSTOMER FEEDBACK Includes comment cards and feedback via your website.	Create as many channels as possible for customers to give you their views. Ask what they think about your products and services, but also seek relevant data about them.
STATUTORY BODIES Regulatory bodies holding data on company performance and finances.	Use statutory sources of information to build a company profile of your typical customer based on factors such as size or turnover. Use this data to target similar companies.

SEGMENTING CUSTOMERS

Break your customer base into segments. You may have low-value regular or occasional customers, or high-value regular or occasional customers. Identify your principal segments and target marketing activity accordingly. High-value customers, for example, may merit more attention, while loyalty programs or discounts may persuade low-value customers to buy more and more often.

15 Turn low-value occasional clients into high-value regular ones.

16 Identify which factors will help you target new customers.

USING THE INFORMATION

Influence your marketing decisions with profiling and segmentation. A profiling exercise might reveal that products aimed at one group are actually bought by another. If a men's underwear company finds that 75 percent of its customers are female, this suggests that men leave their underwear buying to mothers, wives, and girlfriends. In such a case, use mailshots and other advertising to target women, not men.

UNDERSTANDING CUSTOMER BUYING

Find the key to why customers buy and you have unlocked the secret of how to sell to them. Discover what your customers buy, how often, when, and why. Then use this important information to influence your marketing decisions.

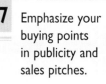

17 Emphasize your buying points in publicity and sales pitches.

18 Ensure that both buying and selling points coincide.

IDENTIFYING SELLING POINTS

A selling point is a powerful factor that you identify internally as helping to clinch a sale. To determine your strongest selling points, you must understand what a customer looks for when making a purchase. This is known as a buying point. To ensure success, the points you highlight when selling should be the same factors that customers most value when buying. You may, for example, decide that being "established for a century" is a good selling point because your company takes pride in this. But your customers' key buying point is likely to be quite different.

◄ ANALYZING BUYING
In a large shopping mall, where stores compete for the same customers, those that promote customers' key buying points – such as good prices – as their selling points are more likely to succeed.

UNDERSTANDING THE BUYING PROCESS

KEY STAGES	CUSTOMER ACTION
RECOGNITION Becoming aware of a need.	Prospective customer realizes that something is required: more space at home, for example.
APPRAISAL Investigating what is available to fulfill need.	Customer reads brochures, magazine articles, looks for information on price, durability, etc.
NEGOTIATION Approaching supplier of product or service.	Having made a choice, customer asks supplier for quotations, looks at warranties, etc.
PURCHASE Buying preferred option.	A decision is made and the customer goes ahead with purchase.
RECOMMENDATION Commending product or service to others.	Customer evaluates the product and, if happy, recommends it to friends, colleagues, etc.

BEING ADAPTABLE

If your customer is a company, as opposed to an individual, bear in mind that its buying process will probably be very specific. This means that to succeed in selling to a company, particularly a business customer, you must understand what its buying process is and adapt your approach to suit. Ask the following questions:

- "Do you consult a list of approved suppliers? If so, how can we get on that list?"
- "Do you ask for tenders? If so, how can we get on the tender list?"
- "Do you always shop around for the best deal?"
- "Do you go by recommendation or use contacts?"
- "Do you always use the same supplier? What would persuade you to try a different one?"

Time spent getting to know how other people's customers buy is time invested in learning how to turn them into your own customers.

QUESTIONS TO ASK YOURSELF

Q How often do our customers buy?

Q What is the average transaction size?

Q Which payment methods do they use?

Q Which customers are most profitable?

Q Which customers are least profitable?

19 When dealing with a company, find out who influences key buying decisions.

USING SURVEYS

Work out some reasons why customers might choose to buy goods or services from you, then use survey techniques to discover the facts. Ask customers to rank the factors you have identified in order of importance, as well as adding their own. Your list might include:

- quick or free delivery;
- competitive price;
- excellent after-sales support;
- easy payment terms;
- friendly staff.

Self-completion questionnaires are an excellent way of reaching customers quickly and cheaply.

20 Collate buying information as an ongoing task.

21 Set a deadline to encourage the return of mailed questionnaires.

MAKING THE MOST OF SURVEY TECHNIQUES

TECHNIQUE	USING IT EFFECTIVELY
MAILED QUESTIONNAIRE An excellent way of reaching a large number of geographically dispersed customers quickly and cheaply.	● Boost return rates by enclosing a stamped self-addressed envelope and use a follow-up mailing to encourage nonresponding customers. ● Make sure that questionnaires have an attractive layout and, above all, are easy to complete.
ONE-TO-ONE INTERVIEW Although time consuming, this is seen as the best type of survey and tends to elicit the best response rate.	● Look at location options carefully: would interviews in the street serve your purpose better than interviews in a hotel, or in your customers' homes or workplaces? ● Rapport is important, so ensure that interviewers explain the purpose and value of the survey.
CUSTOMER PANEL Comprises a group of your customers with a strong interest in your organization or products.	● Use customer panels as a sounding board for new ideas, and a source of valuable feedback. ● Ensure that panels retain their objectivity: if they become too integral a part of the organization's structure, customers can feel more like employees.
FOCUS GROUP A small discussion group led by a facilitator. Its aim is to uncover attitudes, motivations, and qualitative insights.	● Ensure that focus group members are representative of your customers and that the facilitator encourages them to add their input. ● Remember that, although structured, these should be less rigid than questionnaire-based interviews.

UNDERSTANDING MOTIVATION

Usually there will be a combination of several motivating factors to buy, not just one. Easy payment terms might prove to be the clinching factor, but friendliness of staff, or the availability of the product from stock, may also influence the decision to buy from you. It is important to learn what motivates your customers and find ways to build on this knowledge.

MOTIVATING FACTORS ▶

These three customers frequent the same bar, although their reasons for doing so are very different. Being able to identify the principal selling points allows for more effective marketing.

Phil is a regular because the bar serves an extensive range of quality French wines

Tracy uses the bar because it is convenient, just two minutes' walk from her office

Aziz travels some distance to the bar because it has a no-smoking policy

CALCULATING LIFETIME VALUE

Use a simple formula to calculate roughly what the average regular customer is worth to you during your relationship. You can then decide whether to treat high-value customers in a special way, for example by inviting them to special events. The example here shows that although the average sale is only $40, the customer is, in fact, worth $3,200 to the company.

A Value of average sale (divide annual sales in $s by number of transactions)	$40
B Number of transactions each regular customer makes annually	4
C Average number of years a customer buys from you	5
D Average number of referrals/recommendations a customers makes annually	3
E Sales per customer per year (A x B)	$160
F Sales per customer over a lifetime (E x C)	$800
G Potential gross sales from referrals (F x D)	$2,400
TOTAL VALUE OF CUSTOMER (F + G)	**$3,200**

Building Relationships

Selling to existing customers is far cheaper and easier than finding new ones. Use marketing to nurture customer loyalty through good service and quality products, backed up by a strong, lasting, mutually rewarding relationship.

22 Examine every area of customer service and seek to improve it.

Monitoring for Quality of Service

Review all aspects of your working practices

⬇

Set measurable standards so that quality is not left to chance

⬇

Make sure that staff are trained to be able to meet standards

⬇

If necessary, issue staff with a customer service manual

⬇

Measure performance to check that quality is being attained

⬇

Review standards to keep improving customer care

Delivering Service

Customers today expect first-class service, and rightly so. Think about how you felt when you last received poor service. Disappointed? Angry? Cheated? This is exactly how your customers feel when they experience similar treatment. Compare this with how you feel when you receive exceptional service. Remember that customers are not an irritation standing in the way of you and your work, they are your work. Without them you have no business. List areas where you feel that you can improve customer service. Look at how staff interact with customers, how orders are processed, and how correspondence is dealt with. Tackle each area for improvement in turn.

Questions to Ask Yourself

Q Do we answer the phones quickly and courteously?

Q Are our staff neat, helpful, friendly, and knowledgeable?

Q Are our premises clean and comfortable?

Q Do we reply to mail promptly?

Q Do we provide good after-sales service?

Q How swiftly are orders processed?

Q Could we do more to eliminate ordering errors?

Q How many compliments or complaints do we receive?

TACKLING COMPLAINTS

Complaints should always be taken seriously. Some companies have found that customers who have complained, and have had their complaints dealt with to their satisfaction, are more loyal than customers who have never complained. This underlines the importance of handling complaints well. Devise a fair and efficient procedure, set timescales for responding to complaints, and never let a complaint drift on. If you are in the wrong, admit it, apologize, and, if necessary, compensate the customer. Learn from errors and revise procedures so that mistakes are not repeated.

23 Remember that an existing client is more valuable than a potential one.

24 Ask dissatisfied customers how you can win them back.

▼ RESOLVING COMPLAINTS

This illustration shows two outcomes following a customer complaint. When the case is handled badly, the customer not only feels poorly treated enough to take her business elsewhere, but discusses her bad experience with others. When prompt remedial action is taken, the customer feels that her business is valued. Fair, courteous treatment also helps to ensure her continued loyalty.

Customer feels satisfied with the way the complaint has been resolved and is happy to leave her business where it is

Staff member takes call from customer who complains that her order has been delivered late

Staff member apologizes and promises an immediate investigation

Offers to refund 50 percent of the invoiced amount

Puts complaint to one side and forgets all about it

Staff member acts defensively but agrees to look into complaint

Unhappy customer tells everyone about the poor service she has received and takes her business elsewhere

KEEPING IN TOUCH

When a customer places an order, it is not the end of selling, it is just the beginning. Turn that onetime purchase into repeat sales by developing a relationship with your customers. Relationships do not sustain themselves. They take effort, and all the responsibility lies with you. Your customer may not even want a relationship. You have to take the initiative, not them. Find ways to remind customers that you are there. Tell them when their maintenance contract is due for renewal, offer them upgrades, invite them to exclusive previews, give them special discounts, and make sure they are among the first to hear about new developments. Devise valid reasons for communicating and so keep your company's products or services fresh in their minds.

THINGS TO DO

1. Call customers with news and developments.

2. If you cannot get in touch with customers by phone, send an email.

3. Drop in on business clients, if necessary, having checked first that your visit will be convenient for them.

4. Devise new ways of keeping customers informed of special offers or events, sales, and improvements in service.

25 Maintain healthy relationships with customers by being helpful and pleasant at all times.

▼ **USING CUSTOMER CONTACT CARDS**

Sustain relationships by mapping out planned customer contact. Keep records of the contact made with each customer, any follow-up required, and the outcome.

Customer contact card

Customer name: Thelma Driver, Trepark Limited

Due	Action	Completed	Outcome
April 21st	Call to check that new system is working well	✔	System working well. Agreed to meet for lunch
May 3rd	Call to arrange date for lunch	✔	Met and discussed new projects. Have promised to send free tickets to the next trade exhibition
July 16th	Send complimentary tickets to the trade exhibition	✔	Thelma visited trade exhibition with Trevor James, a friend from Davis Company. Have added Trevor's details to mailing list
August 20th	Send copy of customer newsletter	✔	

TESTING THE STRENGTH OF RELATIONSHIPS

There are two tests of a relationship's strength: is a customer satisfied enough to remain loyal?, and is a customer happy to recommend you to others? Find out by asking them. A good way to elicit honest answers is to use a questionnaire, or try an after-sales phone call to customers. Some companies ask these questions on the product warranty registration card. If customers plan to use a different company next time, or are unwilling to recommend you, discover why.

> **26** Thank people for their business to make them feel valued – the human touch can make all the difference.

NURTURING LOYALTY

Customers need a reason to remain loyal. They may expect more than simply excellent products or services. How do your competitors nurture customer loyalty? Could you introduce ways to show customers actively how much you value their business? Loyalty or reward programs have been proven to work for many businesses. Give people a card that records their business with you. After a number of transactions, or after reaching a certain total, they can qualify for special treatment, free gifts, discounts, or other perks. In a competitive market, where customers tend to shop around for the best deal, a voucher offering a reduction off their next order can help attract repeat business. A discount that escalates with each order, while still making a profit for you, might make you irresistible to otherwise fickle customers.

ADVOCATE
If really happy, client becomes an advocate who recommends you to others

CLIENT
If happy, the customer makes repeat purchases and becomes a regular client

CUSTOMER
New customer makes a onetime purchase

PROSPECT
Prospective customer is considering buying, possibly from you, or possibly from a rival

TARGET
Target customer receives information (advertising, sales visit, or other)

UNKNOWN
Unknown customer is not familiar with your company or products

▲ MOVING PEOPLE UP THE LOYALTY LADDER
Successful marketing can turn a casual customer into a committed advocate of your company. Aim to advance everyone to the top of the loyalty ladder.

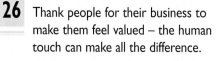

WINNING NEW CUSTOMERS

Customer loss is inevitable: people move, change jobs, and, of course, they die. Losses may be gradual and easy to overlook, but the effects are cumulative. Maintain a thriving business by finding new customers faster than you lose them.

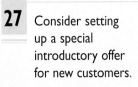

27 Consider setting up a special introductory offer for new customers.

28 Provide incentives to your sales team to help them improve their overall selling performances.

UNDERSTANDING CUSTOMER LOSS

You are sure to be losing some customers, even if you have a full order book. But is this due to natural loss, or could you be driving customers away? Contact former customers and ask them. If losses are due to your own underperformance, take action to correct it. If your traditional customer base appears to be a dying breed, your business is heading for terminal decline. The only cure is to find a new market and possibly also to develop new products or services. Replacing customers is an endless task, but an essential one.

FINDING NEW BUSINESS

It is vital to go out and find customers, since they cannot be relied upon to come to you. Plan how you are going to win new business. Follow up all leads and get in touch with people who have made an inquiry or requested information. Contact former customers in a bid to win them back. Identify potential customers and let them know how you can help. Approach competitors' customers and make them a better offer. Review your publicity strategy to see if there is a better way of reaching potential customers. Would cold calling or a direct mail campaign be useful in attracting new business?

QUESTIONS TO ASK YOURSELF

● Do we know how many customers we lose?

● Do we know the reasons why customers desert us?

● Are there any compelling reasons why customers should remain loyal to us?

● How do we show our customers that we value them and their loyalty?

● Could we do more to retain our customers?

INCREASING YOUR CUSTOMER BASE

There is a well-established technique, known as member-get-member, or MGM, that many businesses use to good effect in the endless challenge to win new business. Try to get each of your existing customers to provide just one productive lead. You can literally double the size of your customer base using this method; but obviously your customers will be willing to participate only if they feel happy with your products and your organization generally. Use incremental incentives to encourage customers to provide leads.

▼ TURNING CUSTOMERS INTO YOUR SALES FORCE

Happy customers can do as good a job for you as the most highly trained sales force, and at a fraction of the cost. Harness the enthusiasm of satisfied customers and ask them to help you spread the word to their friends and family. An easy-to-complete card sent to regulars can result in valuable leads.

USING INCENTIVES

Ask customers for details of colleagues/friends who might like to be on your mailing list

Offer a small incentive, such as a prize drawing, to encourage customers to supply leads

Send your mailing to leads, explaining that a friend recommended them

If necessary, offer a bigger incentive, such as a free gift, if a lead places an order

---

Highlight the incentive in the headline

RECOMMEND US AND ENTER OUR PRIZE DRAWiING

As a loyal customer you already know how great our products are. Don't keep it a secret! If you have friends or family who might like to find out what we have to offer, please include their details, and we will make sure they receive a copy of our latest catalog free of charge. In return for your help, we will enter you into our PRIZE DRAW for the opportunity to win a case of champagne. If your friend goes on to place an order with us, we will also send you a COMPLIMENTARY BOX OF CHOCOLATES as a thank you.

You may want to ask customers for additional details, but remember that the more information you ask them for, the less likely they are to respond

Your name and address:

Your friend's name and address:

Include your address on the card just in case the prepaid envelope is lost

Please return this card, in the prepaid envelope, by March 30th to qualify for the prize drawing. Send to Garden Tools Limited, Unit 17, Anytown Business Park, Anytown, US.

Make the incentive incremental, with a small incentive for supplying details and a larger one if the prospective customer places an order

Make it easy for respondents to reply by, for example, using prepaid envelopes

Include a reply-by date to encourage customers to act

BUILDING STRONG PRODUCTS

Quality products, backed by a strong brand, are vital for success. To keep your customers and stay ahead of competitors, you must develop first-class new products and improve existing ones.

IMPROVING PRODUCTS

Products generally have some kind of life cycle: some age and die, while others need restyling to remain fresh. Change, enhance, repackage, rebrand, remodel, or upgrade your products to ensure that they appeal to today's market.

 29 Tell former customers about improvements to your products.

 30 Use comment cards to elicit useful feedback.

31 Regard feedback from customers as valuable marketing intelligence.

ENHANCING PRODUCTS

Before investing considerable time and effort in developing new products, look at your current line. It is important to avoid creating new products at the expense of existing ones. For the best ideas on how to improve your products, consult the experts: your customers. Seek their opinions and suggestions using questionnaires, comment cards, focus groups, or customer panels, so that you can introduce real enhancements based on customer demand. Keep products fresh by introducing new variants, limited editions, add-ons, special recipes, and improved versions.

32 Always look for ways to improve your products.

33 Always thank your customers for their comments, even if they are negative.

PROMOTING PRODUCT IMPROVEMENTS

Whenever you introduce product improvements, tell your customers. You can use this as an excuse to write, telephone, or visit them. Ensure that your ads mention the enhancements, and use product packaging to draw attention to them. You can also highlight improvements in your publicity material. Brief your sales team on new features so that they are able to promote them. If there is a news angle, issue a press release to attract positive media coverage. Significant improvements to products will provide a launchpad for renewed promotional activity aimed at reviving sales.

LEARNING FROM YOUR COMPETITORS

Study your competitors; you may find that some of their ideas or working practices are worth copying or adapting. As a member of the public, sample any improvements they make to their products and services. Send for their publicity material. Phone their switchboard. Read their advertisements. Visit at one of their outlets. Examine organizations in other sectors. Is there anything they can teach you? Which of their good ideas are transferable or adaptable? Be on the lookout for ideas that you can adopt, adapt, borrow, or steal. Aim to improve existing products by taking the best of the rest and incorporating them to create a product that cannot be beaten.

Colleague checks competitor's website

▼ MONITORING COMPETING PRODUCTS

An easy way to compare your product with rival products is to search the internet and see what other companies are offering. Make sure you monitor the competition periodically, not just once.

Manager looks at competitor's brochure

DIFFERENTIATING YOUR PRODUCTS

*F*ew products are unique. Often the challenge lies in finding a way to differentiate your products from a rival's near-identical offerings. Make use of a combination of techniques to give you an advantage over the competition.

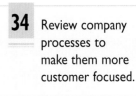

34 Review company processes to make them more customer focused.

35 Ask customers what your unique selling point is.

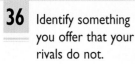

36 Identify something you offer that your rivals do not.

UNDERSTANDING COMPETITIVE EDGE

When your products are better than those of your competitors, and when customers recognize this superiority, you have a real advantage. Few organizations are in this position. Most find that there is little or nothing to distinguish their own products from a competitor's. To gain competitive advantage, uncover not just differences but also attributes that customers value. Make sure the differences are meaningful to customers, so that your product is preferable to the others available.

RECOGNIZING WHAT IS IMPORTANT

Often it is the little things that count. Customers may choose your product over a competitor's identical product simply because they prefer your packaging, or because you give them coffee while they wait. Pay attention to details that could make a difference. A genuine customer-centric approach will differentiate you from competitors. Show your commitment to customers and ensure that staff are empathic. Review company systems and processes to make them more customer focused.

QUESTIONS TO ASK YOURSELF

Q Why should customers buy from us rather than from our competitors?

Q What makes us different from our competitors?

Q How are we better than our rivals?

Q What strengths do we have that we can effectively capitalize on?

ADDING VALUE

When there is nothing intrinsically different about your product, look to your strengths as an organization to find your competitive edge. A combination of the following may differentiate you from your rivals:

● free/same-day delivery
● products held in stock
● free trial
● on-site demonstration of product
● choice of payment terms/ interest-free credit
● free parking
● personal service from trained staff
● better warranty
● good after-sales service/ on-site repairs
● 1–800 customer helpline

37 Gain advantage over your competitors by achieving total customer satisfaction.

IDENTIFYING USPs

Even an indistinguishable product can have a claim to uniqueness, and you may still have a unique selling point (USP). Perhaps you are the only local company to offer such a service, or were the first to make it available. You may be the newest, the nearest, or the largest. You might be the most experienced, the only family-owned firm, or the longest-established. Perhaps you are the only supplier to have achieved a coveted award, or maybe your staff have all reached a certain level of training or experience. Scrutinize your company for a claim to uniqueness. Check that none of your competitors is making a similar claim. Even a weakness can be turned into a strength. Being the smallest, for example, could be a USP. It means that you can offer a more personal, flexible service.

◀ **CREATING AN ADVANTAGE**
By differentiating her own business from her near-identical neighboring competitor, Vanessa succeeded in making her florist's shop far more profitable. Her idea was simple but clever: adding value for customers without increasing cost. Creative thinking is free, but can result in significant business gains.

CASE STUDY

Vanessa and Susan ran two flower shops, which were situated only a short distance apart on the same street. Both florists had to compete for the same customers, and since their stock and prices were similar, there was no strong reason for customers to favor one florist over the other. Searching for a way to increase business, Vanessa came up with the idea of making special bouquets to coordinate with interior color schemes. It was not more expensive for Vanessa to offer this new service, nor did customers have to pay any more to use it, yet the scheme gave Vanessa the competitive advantage she was looking for. Customers were delighted and made a point of returning to Vanessa's shop rather than to her rival's. Just over a year later, the shop managed by Susan closed, increasing Vanessa's business even further.

PROVIDING INCENTIVES

Even without uniqueness you can still build a competitive edge. Ask yourself, "Why would a customer choose us rather than one of our competitors?" If you cannot come up with at least one compelling reason, consider using incentives. These can encourage customers to opt for you over a rival. Be sure to work out costs and benefits very carefully before taking this route. If you offer an expensive incentive, you or your customer will end up paying the price; it needs to be cheap to you but attractive to the customer. Choose a relevant incentive, such as a free tie with every suit, or free on-site servicing with every photocopier.

UNDERSTANDING THE BUYING PROCESS

Select incentive

Discard incentive

Will incentive persuade customer to buy from you rather than from a competitor?
YES   NO

Will incentive result in a boost to sales sufficient to cover extra costs incurred?
YES   NO

Go ahead with incentive and carefully monitor results

38 Choose an incentive that will enhance your reputation; tawdry gifts may tarnish your image.

SEEKING ENDORSEMENTS

Endorsements can be powerful persuaders, providing customers with a strong reason to buy from you. Who could resist saucepans promoted as the professional cook's favorite? Or the home computer that programmers choose? Or the vacation resort where travel agents take their vacation? Customers like the safety and security that an endorsement provides. A relevant endorsement can result in a dramatic sales boost.

CULTURAL DIFFERENCES

Before using endorsements and testimonials, check the relevant legislation. In the United States, the Federal Trade Commission regulates the use of endorsements and testimonials in advertising. Strict rules apply to any advertising message that consumers are likely to believe reflects the opinions, findings, or experience of a third party other than the sponsoring advertiser.

USING TESTIMONIALS

Testimonials serve exactly the same purpose as endorsements, but the difference between them is that a testimonial quotes a named person who has used the product and wishes to recommend it. Famous faces, relevant professionals and experts, and even ordinary people can provide testimonials. Customers are more likely to believe third-party testimony than to accept your company's claims of excellence. Testimonials reproduced in your publicity material in a handwritten form appear to be more persuasive and believable than typewritten ones. Always get written consent before using any testimonial, and make sure that the views expressed in it can be supported by independent evidence.

 39 Ensure that views expressed in testimonials can be supported.

40 Choose an incentive that is relevant to the product.

 **41** Brief your sales team to highlight product benefits, not features, when talking to customers.

EVALUATING FEATURES AND BENEFITS

When promoting products, companies have a tendency to focus attention on a product's features. But customers do not look for features; they want to see benefits. Regard features merely as a way of creating benefits. Start by listing the features for each of your products and then add the benefits that customers derive from them. Make sure that all your publicity material and packaging highlights the latter.

COMPARING FEATURES AND BENEFITS

FEATURE	BENEFIT
"Uses the latest microchip technology"	"Never again burn a slice of toast"
"Built-in moisture reader"	"Transforms stale bread into fresh toast"
"Audible toast-completion alert"	"Bell lets you know when the toast is ready"

DEVELOPING A BRAND

*S*trong, well-known products provide
companies with a real competitive
advantage. Use the power of branding to
imbue your products with personality and
meaning, ensuring they achieve a prominent
position in the marketplace.

> **42** Establish trust in
> your brand and
> customers will
> remain loyal.

NAMING PRODUCTS

The right name helps to sell products and services.
It bestows individuality and personality, enabling
customers to identify with your offerings and to
get to know them. It makes products and services
tangible and real. Choose names that enhance your
company image and that are appropriate for the
product and its positioning in the marketplace.
Check that the name is available and register it so
that it cannot be used by others. If your market
is international, ensure that the name is
pronounceable in other languages and does not
translate into a vulgar word or one with negative
connotations. Aim for a name that is short, apt,
easy to spell, and memorable. Strict rules
govern the naming of
organizations, so check
them out with the
relevant official body.

▼ **TESTING YOUR
BRAND NAME**
*Show your shortlist of product names to
target customers and ask them what
images each name conjures up. Use their
feedback to help select a name with the
most positive associations.*

*International customer
considers whether names
will be appropriate in
her country*

*Regional customer
rejects two names
because they have
negative connotations
in her area*

*Target customer
gives his view on the
appeal of suggested
product names*

COMPARING BRAND ATTRIBUTES

SERVICE ATTRIBUTES	PRODUCT ATTRIBUTES

Friendliness	Durability
Creativity	Reliability
Courtesy	Usefulness
Helpfulness	Value
Knowledgeability	Aesthetic value

43 Extend branding across your entire product line.

Manager asks selected customers for feedback on new product names

HARNESSING BRAND POWER

An effective way of differentiating your products from those of your competitors is to use branding. Branding means developing unique attributes so that your products are instantly recognizable, memorable, and evoke positive associations. Some brands have a solid and reliable personality, others are youthful and fun. Choose your company and product name, corporate colors, logo, packaging, and promotional activity to help convey a personality and build a brand. Branding conveys a complex message quickly. A customer should be able to look at one of your products and assimilate all that you stand for in a second by recalling the brand values.

44 A strong brand is not a substitute for quality, but an enhancement to it.

45 Look out for opportunities to reinforce your corporate identity.

46 Maintain corporate identity consistently by issuing written guidelines for staff.

PROMOTING A CORPORATE IDENTITY

The creation of a corporate identity is a vital element of branding. Present an integrated, strong, instantly recognizable, individual image that is regarded in a positive way by your customers, and seize every opportunity to strengthen your corporate identity. Devise a distinctive logo and corporate colors, and use them on stationery, packaging materials, and on your vehicle. Work the branding into the the design and layout of your premises. Big hotel chains, for example, reinforce their corporate identity through color-coordinated staff uniforms, carpets, soft furnishings, and towels. They also have napkins, coasters, tableware, and cutlery bearing the company logo.

POINTS TO REMEMBER

- A logo forms a central part of your corporate identity and should convey something about your business.
- It may incorporate a baseline – a summary of your mission or your business.
- A logo can be typographical or a design in its own right.
- The logo's colors will become your corporate colors.

▲ CREATING A STRONG IDENTITY

Utilizing distinctive corporate colors and logos on company vehicles helps to build a strong identity. This ensures that an individual company is easily distinguishable from others that may offer very similar services.

47 Be aware that colors can have cultural or political connotations.

48 Keep corporate colors to a minimum to keep printing costs low.

49 Ensure all aspects of company behavior reflect brand values.

COMMISSIONING A VISUAL IDENTITY

If your organization lacks a strong visual identity, or has an outmoded image, consider a restyle. Give a full brief of your brand values and positioning to a graphic designer whose style you like, and ask them to produce some ideas. Explain how you intend to use your new corporate identity. Will it be placed on vehicles, for example, or on storefronts? Ask to see your proposed new visual identity on mock-ups of items on which it will ultimately appear: product packaging, stationery, and so on. Test your shortlisted design on a focus group comprising your key audiences, such as customers and suppliers. Find out what associations it produces. Take time to develop a new identity; you will have to live with it for a long while.

MAINTAINING BRAND VALUES

Having established a brand, work to maintain its positive values. Use patents, trademarks, design rights, and other devices to protect your brand and prevent others from cashing in on its success. Live up to your projected image. Ensure that standards of customer care, service, and product quality remain high, giving real substance to the brand. It can take years to create a successful brand yet seconds to destroy it. Check regularly that the brand values are still relevant, since brands can become outdated. Gently reposition the brand over time where necessary, or opt for a major repositioning and use media exposure to promote your new image.

▼ **GAINING RECOGNITION**
Successful brands have such a strong visual identity that they are instantly recognizable, even when seen in a foreign language. Companies can often charge more for winning brands, since customers feel, often subliminally, more confident in the value of the product.

ACHIEVING GROWTH THROUGH PRODUCTS

Selling more products is the most effective strategy for ensuring big increases in profitability. Achieve growth in this way by expanding your share of the existing market, finding new markets, developing new products, or diversifying.

50 Use the internet as a vehicle for reaching global markets.

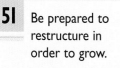
51 Be prepared to restructure in order to grow.

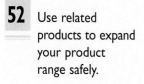
52 Use related products to expand your product range safely.

PENETRATING THE MARKET

One way to ensure growth is to achieve a larger share of the market. This strategy is widely used because it is considered a "safe" way to grow. Security lies in the fact that you are dealing with two known entities: your offerings, i.e. your products, and the market. You have already spent time getting to know this market and refining your products to meet customer need, so you avoid the need to invest in new research, or in new product development. Your goal is simply to make contact with previously unreached potential customers.

DEVELOPING THE MARKET

Market development involves finding new markets for your existing products. Start by drawing up a list of possible new markets. Conduct research to check whether they would be interested in your offerings and that you could satisfy potential new customers with your existing products. Some product remodeling may be necessary if you are to appeal to your new market, but remember that you are not looking at totally new products. Finally, plan how you will reach your new markets.

POINTS TO REMEMBER

- It is possible to increase sales by simple but valued product improvements.
- You may combine, for example, product development with market penetration.
- It is a good idea to develop new products that will be bought in the same transaction as your existing products.

IMPLEMENTING GROWTH STRATEGIES

GROWTH STRATEGY	IMPLEMENTION METHODS
MARKET PENETRATION Improving market share by reaching previously unreached potential customers.	● Use heavy advertising, promotional offers, direct mail campaigns, or cold calling to find new customers matching the profile of existing ones. ● Focus on winning customers from competitors.
MARKET DEVELOPMENT Identifying and breaking into new markets to increase sales of existing products.	● Use targeted advertising, direct mail, and the internet. ● Consider an internal restructuring, such as setting up a sales arm to deal with large companies, or remodel products to appeal to new markets.
PRODUCT DEVELOPMENT Introducing new product lines or add-ons to existing products to appeal to current market.	● Research new product ideas, ask customers for opinions, and examine successful rival product lines. ● Examine your market carefully to ensure that it is not already oversaturated.
DIVERSIFICATION Expanding through the development of new products to be sold to new markets.	● Remember that the rules applying to setting up a new enterprise also apply to organizations seeking to diversify. ● If you decide to diversify, you will need to develop a separate marketing strategy.

CREATING NEW PRODUCTS

Achieve growth and keep risk to a minimum by introducing new product lines to your existing market. Products introduced to an existing line can be very successful. A curtain manufacturer, for example, may add coordinating bedlinen to its line of curtains. Customers will often buy an existing product (a mobile phone) and a new one (a colorful, snap-on cover) in the same transaction.

53 Ask customers what new products they would like to see on the market.

DIVERSIFYING

54 Be sure to explore all the alternatives before risking diversification.

The riskiest growth strategy – diversification – involves developing totally new products to sell to new markets, and it is a journey into the complete unknown. Essentially you are embarking on an undertaking not dissimilar to a complete new business start-up. This is not often a first choice for boosting profits, but it can be – and has been – done. Explore all the alternatives first.

MAXIMIZING PUBLICITY

To buy from you, customers must know what you have to sell, which is why promotion is a vital part of the marketing mix. Learn to make the most of publicity to boost sales and profits.

PLANNING A CAMPAIGN

A successful publicity campaign can lead to an enhanced profile, increased sales, and improved profits. Before embarking on a campaign, map out exactly what you wish to achieve so that you can choose the right method to attain your goals.

 55 Use calendars and desktop giveaways to keep your name in view of clients.

 56 Use directories and annuals as publicity tools.

57 Use launches and previews to reach customers.

SETTING OBJECTIVES

The first step of a publicity campaign is to consider the outcome you desire and then set one or more clear, specific, measurable, time-framed objectives to achieve it. Avoid vague outcomes, such as "to attract more orders," and be explicit, for example, "to attract orders valued at $100,000 within four weeks" or "to attract 5,000 inquiries, leading to 1,000 sales in two months." Only by setting measurable objectives will you be able to identify what works and what does not. This will allow you to concentrate your publicity budget where it will produce the best results.

EVALUATING KEY METHODS

By far the most popular methods of gaining publicity are press and radio advertising, direct mail, and the internet, since these have high impact and are affordable for most businesses. When considering which method to use, bear in mind the following:

- Advertising in print allows excellent targeting, since most publications have detailed readership profiles.
- Radio ads are easier to digest than print ads, but they are more transient.
- Direct mail is highly effective, provided that it is efficiently targeted, although it does have a rather poor image.
- The internet is a booming growth area with a vast potential for publicity.

ORGANIZING A SUCCESSFUL CAMPAIGN

Draw up a profile of your target audience
Do you wish to target one specific group or a wider range of people?

Look at when and how often to reach them
Do you need to contact people at a specific time of day, month, or year?

Select appropriate publicity method(s)
Which method(s) will deliver at the right time and place?

Calculate the cost of your chosen campaign
Examine whether your campaign is likely to achieve set objectives

Ensure systems are in place to handle response
Check that staff levels and stocks are sufficient to meet demand

COMBINING METHODS

The best way to obtain maximum publicity is to organize an integrated campaign combining several methods. This allows optimum penetration of the market: one technique builds upon the work achieved by another. A software company targeting business start-ups, for example, could place a coupon response ad in the national press offering a free business software package to business start-ups. This would bring in names and addresses of target customers, to whom direct mail and publicity could be sent with the free packages.

POINTS TO REMEMBER

- Check that any claims made in your publicity materials can be substantiated.
- Avoid making false or exaggerated claims.
- Ensure publicity is both accurate and unambiguous.
- Be sure that publicity does not mislead or deliberately give the wrong impression.

Getting the Most from Advertising

Advertising is a paid-for, persuasive promotional activity that uses the media and other publicity channels, such as the internet. Use it to build and maintain awareness; to publicize special offers, sales, and events; to promote new products and services; to announce price changes, revised opening hours, or product modifications; to invite inquiries, and to find new customers. Above all, use it to sell. Direct response advertising (incorporating a response device, such as a coupon or fax number) brings you and your customers together.

58 Ensure relevant staff know which ads are appearing when.

CALCULATING COST ▶

Use a simple formula to check that an advertising campaign will produce results. When adding up the total cost of your campaign, include every item, not only the cost of buying space or airtime. If forecast sales exceed the break-even figure (C), success is likely. Allow a margin of error: response rates are a guideline and not a guarantee.

(A) **Total cost of campaign**	$1,000
(B) **Profit per sale**	$20
(C) **Number of sales need to break even** (A) ÷ (B)	**50**
(D) **Mailing quantity, circulation figures, or listening/viewing statistics**	5,000
(E) **Expected response rate** (based on figures supplied by publication/station)	80
FORECAST SALES	**62.5**

Defining the Key Steps to Successful Publicity

Key Steps	How to Tackle them
Grab Attention	Use a striking design, a hard-hitting headline, strong colors, large lettering, powerful photography, or other devices to get noticed.
Hold Interest	Devise an appealing, persuasive proposition that will make potential customers sit up and pay attention.
Stimulate Desire	Make your offer irresistible: show how good the deal is and highlight valuable extras, such as easy payment terms or quick delivery.
Gain Conviction	Convince customers that they need what you are selling by giving powerful reasons that will appeal to them.
Push for Action	Urge customers to act using words such as "time-limited offer." Make action easier with coupons, 1–800 numbers, credit card payment, etc.

USING EXPERTS

If you are planning a major campaign, or intend to move into a specialized area, such as television or movie advertising, consider calling in the experts. Media professionals should be able to run a campaign more effectively on your behalf, and sometimes for less money than you would pay, and usually more quickly. If you plan to spend a lot on advertising, it could be to your advantage to use an advertising agency. Agencies earn a commission for buying media space or airtime, and this may cover their creative and account management costs. This effectively means that you are receiving their services for nothing. Approach a few advertising agencies and find out how they structure their fees.

MAKING IT LEGAL

Strict industry and legal codes govern advertising in the United Kingdom and the United States. In the US, for example, Federal Trade Commission regulations cover advertising, marketing and promotional activities, and sales practices in general. In Canada, the industry adheres to a Code of Advertising Standards. In the UK, over 150 statutes and regulations relate to a host of advertising issues.

59 Investigate using an outside company to handle the extra work for you.

PREPARING TO RESPOND

Be ready for the response to your campaign by ensuring that there are plenty of staff to answer telephone calls as well as process, pack, and dispatch orders. Organize extra telephone lines, if necessary. Check that you have sufficient stock, packaging materials, brochures, or information packs to fulfill responses. Delays will reflect badly on your company and may lead to customer loss. If you cannot cope with a big response, stagger your advertising. Target one geographic area or customer group, fulfill orders, then place your next batch of advertisements. Alternatively, employ a specialized fulfillment house to handle all the extra work on your behalf.

◀ BEING PREPARED

Be ready for the increase in customer response once your marketing takes effect. If necessary, employ more telephone staff and ensure that they are fully briefed.

ADVERTISING IN PRINT

Press advertising offers the cheapest way to reach a large audience and is highly effective for direct response advertising, where the public buys straight off the page. Choose the right publication, craft your ads carefully, and negotiate the best deal.

 60 Bear in mind that spaces between paragraphs will increase readership.

 61 Avoid too much small print; it is difficult to read.

 62 Keep your idea or proposition as simple as possible.

REQUESTING MEDIA KITS

Draw up a list of possible publications in which to advertise and ask each one to send a media kit, with information on readership profiles and circulation details. Choose the best title for your product and target audience. Details and dates of special features contained in the kit will help you to decide the best time to place your ad. Try to book space for the time when your chosen publication is running a feature on your market sector. The kit will set out the deadlines for placing an ad, as well as technical data explaining the form in which to supply artwork.

NEGOTIATING THE BEST PRICE

Never agree to pay the quoted rate card price for advertising space without first trying to negotiate it down. It is almost always possible to arrange some kind of reduction. Various factors affect cost, including the time of year, demand, the size and position of your ad, circulation of the publication, and whether the ad is in black type or color. If demand for space is slack, a discount is usually available. Even if you cannot get the price reduced, try to negotiate a bigger ad for the same price, a second ad at half price, or a more prominent position for it.

QUESTIONS TO ASK YOURSELF

Q What do we hope to achieve as a result of advertising?

Q Whom do we want to reach, and what do we want to say to them?

Q Which publications do our target customers read?

Q How often do we need to advertise to get our message across successfully?

Q How large will our ad need to be?

USING THE RIGHT PUBLICATION

TYPE OF PUBLICATION	ADVANTAGES AND DISADVANTAGES
FREE LOCAL PAPERS Usually weekly, these contain editorials on the local area and are delivered free through the door.	● These rely solely on advertising for income, so there are many more ads competing for attention. ● It is cheap to advertise in these papers and easier to get away with less sophisticated ads.
"PAID-FOR" PAPERS Daily and weekly, local and regional, these are generally paid-for titles serving local cities and communities.	● Good for local organizations, or national ones, wishing to target areas where they have outlets. ● Short lead-in times. ● Daily papers have a short shelf life.
NATIONAL NEWSPAPERS These are daily publications, usually with a Sunday edition.	● Good for reaching a mass audience since readership profiles allow wide socioeconomic targeting. ● National advertising can be prestigious. ● Expensive and with a short shelf life.
CONSUMER MAGAZINES This huge range of publications includes women's, lifestyle, music, health, and sports titles.	● Good for targeting special interest groups. ● High reader interest so more likely to be read. ● Longer lead-in times. ● Competitors are likely to be advertising in them, too.
PROFESSIONAL PUBLICATIONS These include publications for particular professions and trades, from architects to pig farmers.	● Excellent for targeting a particular professional group. ● Often retained for reference, extending their shelf life. ● Often passed around the workplace and read by more than one person.

TARGETING ADS ▶

Andrew found that advertising in the wrong place produced no new leads, whereas a well-placed advertisement generated a steady stream of new work. He learned that an advertising campaign in itself will not necessarily produce an upturn in sales. For his ads to be effective, they needed to reach the right target. Readership profiles helped him to pinpoint the right publication – the one that was read by his potential customers.

CASE STUDY

Andrew ran an architectural practice in a large city, working on domestic projects. He first advertised in an architectural magazine but realized that it was the wrong vehicle for him, since only those in the trade were reading it. Andrew then drew up a profile of the clients he wanted to reach: reasonably well-off people who lived within a 50-mile radius of the city in which he practiced. He placed an ad in the regional glossy lifestyle magazine for his area. The readership profile stated that the magazine was bought by relatively affluent property owners interested in homes and interiors, and they all lived within reach of the city. The profile was perfect. Andrew's first ad produced 15 inquiries, which led to nine commissions. He decided to advertise there monthly and gained 80 percent of his work this way. As a result, turnover increased by 60 percent.

WRITING A PRESS AD

Make sure that the elements making up your ad – style of language, tone, colors, graphics, photographs, and illustrations – are chosen with your target reader in mind. Check competitors' ads, too, to see how they promote their products. Do you want to take a similar approach, or a radically different one? Create a clear, simple proposition, and avoid complex ideas that require hard work from readers. Ensure that all the elements of your ad work in harmony. Use text to reinforce any photos or illustrations, and eye-catching design to hold the various aspects together, thereby creating an unmissable and persuasive ad that makes readers act.

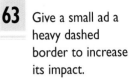

63 Give a small ad a heavy dashed border to increase its impact.

▼ **MAKING YOUR PRESS AD WORK**
When readers see an ad for the first time, their eye follows a set route. Take account of this route when designing your ad. Readers tend to look first at the picture, then at the headline, bottom right-hand corner, captions, subheads, and body copy, in that order.

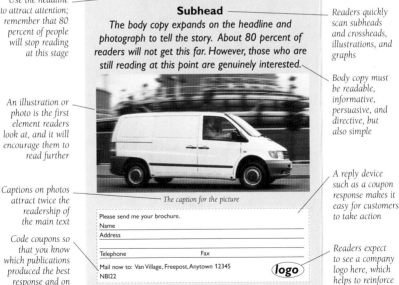

Use the headline to attract attention; remember that 80 percent of people will stop reading at this stage

MAIN HEADING
Subhead
The body copy expands on the headline and photograph to tell the story. About 80 percent of readers will not get this far. However, those who are still reading at this point are genuinely interested.

Readers quickly scan subheads and crossheads, illustrations, and graphs

Body copy must be readable, informative, persuasive, and directive, but also simple

An illustration or photo is the first element readers look at, and it will encourage them to read further

The caption for the picture

Captions on photos attract twice the readership of the main text

Please send me your brochure.
Name
Address
Telephone   Fax
Mail now to: Van Village, Freepost, Anytown 12345
NBI22

logo

A reply device such as a coupon response makes it easy for customers to take action

Code coupons so that you know which publications produced the best response and on which days

Readers expect to see a company logo here, which helps to reinforce corporate identity

PRETESTING ADS

Before spending your budget on buying media space, ask your staff, passers-by in the street, or, best of all, your target audience what they think of your ads. Discover whether they find the ads attractive, the copy readable, and the proposition persuasive. See which of two ads they like best. Both ads might be yours; or one could be your competitor's. After the ads have appeared, you can then assess their effectiveness using objective measures, such as the number of inquiries generated, the number of sales, or the percentage upturn in people through your doors. Measuring outcomes can occur only after an ad has been placed.

 64 Appeal directly to readers by using the "first person" in advertising copy.

65 Use color ads to attract twice the readership of mono ones.

ANALYZING DIFFERENT TYPES OF HEADLINE

HEADLINE TYPE	EXAMPLE	WHEN TO USE IT
DIRECT Presents your proposition in a direct and concise form.	"Any van serviced for just $80 at Van Village"	To present a simple proposition requiring little or no explanatory body copy.
FILTER Shows the relevance of your ad by flagging up the target audience.	"Attention all van owners"	To attract the right prospective customers and ensure that they do not overlook your ad.
CRYPTIC Attracts the reader's curiosity but makes no sense as a stand-alone headline.	"It's what everyone's talking about"	To hook your readers and lure them into your body copy, providing you with an opportunity to persuade them.
COMMAND Issues the reader with an instruction that cannot be ignored.	"Contact us today to arrange your cheap van service"	To prompt readers to take action and respond to your ad.
QUESTION Poses a query to which the answer should be "yes."	"Want to save money servicing your van?"	To engage readers' interest and push them toward accepting your proposition.

ADVERTISING ON RADIO

Since customers listen to the radio at home, at work, and in their cars, it is an effective way of plugging your message. Weigh up the pros and cons of using local and national commercial radio, investigate what is involved, and carefully assess costs.

66 Find out if the radio station can help with production.

67 Ask to listen to ads that agencies have already produced.

MAKING GOOD ADS

The most successful radio ads induce listeners to prick up their ears. Sound, music, voices, accents, both a male and a female voice for extra rhythm, and a conversational style in which speakers talk directly to the listener are all elements of a good ad. Since a studio and specialized equipment are needed, appoint an advertising agency, or commission the radio station's in-house creative team to script and produce the ad for you. Look at the station's listener profile and think of a real person you know who fits that profile. Try the ad out on them. Would they like it? Would they be persuaded to buy?

QUIZZING A STATION REPRESENTATIVE ▼

Have a list of questions ready to ask the representative. Find out what the listener profile is, whether it changes at night, and what costs are involved. Remember that the representative wants to sell airtime to you, so may be economical with the truth.

Radio representative provides information about the station and its listeners

Manager asks questions from a prepared list

Colleague notes facts and sales points

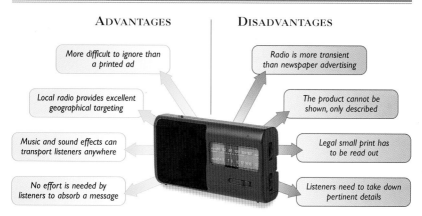

ADVANTAGES

More difficult to ignore than a printed ad

Local radio provides excellent geographical targeting

Music and sound effects can transport listeners anywhere

No effort is needed by listeners to absorb a message

DISADVANTAGES

Radio is more transient than newspaper advertising

The product cannot be shown, only described

Legal small print has to be read out

Listeners need to take down pertinent details

PLANNING COSTS

There is more to radio advertising than buying airtime, so it is important to budget for extra costs. You may need to pay a copywriter to write the script for your ad, as well as actors or voice-over artists. If you commission your own music or jingle, you will need to pay a composer, musicians, and singers. Existing music will require permission to play and involves airplay royalties. Studio time, technicians, and sound effects all have a cost, too.

▲ **WEIGHING UP THE BENEFITS**
Consider both the pros and cons of radio advertising. You may find that spreading your advertising budget over a range of mediums will be more effective.

68 Remember that radio ads are heard, not seen.

ADVERTISING ON TELEVISION

It is possible to produce radio ads without using an advertising agency, but television advertising is far more specialized and technical. Commission an agency to advise on where, when, and how to advertise, as well as coming up with creative ideas and overseeing production. Contact at least three agencies with a written brief explaining what you wish to achieve. Ask each to do a presentation outlining their credentials, explaining how they would approach your assignment, and detailing costs. Look at examples of their work and ask for their client list. Select your agency on their experience and ability, creativity and approach to the campaign, their understanding of your needs, enthusiasm, and total cost.

MASTERING DIRECT MAIL

Direct mail is a form of advertising that delivers targeted, individually addressed communications through the mail. Select the contents of your mailshot carefully, ensure it hits its target, then test the effectiveness of the campaign.

69 Make sure you keep your mailing list up to date at all times.

70 Ensure that people's names are correctly spelled.

IDENTIFYING USES

Direct mail has many marketing applications. Use it to find and convert new prospects, to distribute product samples or newsletters, and as a selling tool targeting current customers. Launch new products, win back lapsed customers, and announce changes to your service or forthcoming sales, events, and special offers – all via the post. Use the technique to build and maintain customer relationships. Keep in touch with clients, send them Christmas cards, tell them all the latest news and developments. Send out questionnaires and gather valuable marketing information.

UNDERSTANDING DIRECT MAIL ▼

Direct mail is a carefully targeted mailshot sent only to people with a proclivity to buy the product or service being promoted. Junk mail is irrelevant mail sent to the wrong people.

DIRECT MAIL RECIPIENT

JUNK MAIL RECIPIENT

A regular skier, recipient reads about promotion offering cut-price skiing equipment with great interest

Recipient has never skied, has no intention of doing so, and barely glances at the mailshot

TARGETING YOUR MAILSHOT

Your mailshot is only as good as the address printed on it, which is why a good mailing list is essential if you are to target customers effectively and maximize your returns. Mailing to people who have moved or changed jobs, who hate direct mail, or who are just not interested is a waste of your marketing budget. Existing customers are three times as likely to respond to a mailing as cold prospects, so make them the basis of your list and then start looking for names to add. People who have inquired in the past and former customers could be worth testing, as could people whose business cards you have collected.

71 Write "you" in your mailshots; it is a powerful lure.

CULTURAL DIFFERENCES

Some countries operate mailing, telephone, and fax preference programs that allow consumers to opt-out of receiving direct mail, so-called "junk" faxes, and cold calling on the telephone. Before embarking on a direct mail campaign, check the legislation and codes that affect direct mail in your country, including any laws relating to the use of information on databases.

POINTS TO REMEMBER

● Direct mail is particularly effective for targeting specific customer types.

● Accurate measuring of direct mail's effectiveness is easy.

● Some recipients dislike direct mail and will not open anything that might be a mailshot.

● A mailshot can be undertaken entirely in-house.

● Mailshots can be used for direct selling, thus cutting out the middleman and saving money.

RENTING A LIST

When seeking new customers, you may wish to approach a list broker who can provide names and addresses of people who match the profile of your existing customers. Note that mailing lists are usually rented, not bought; you buy permission to use the list a certain number of times. If you attempt to use it more often, be warned: brokers plant "seed" names to check that their lists are not reused without permission. The names you rent are called "cold prospects." However, if they respond to your mailing, they become "warm prospects" and you can legitimately add them to your own mailing list and contact them again. Make sure you ask the broker the following questions:
● How was the list compiled?
● When was the list last updated?
● How has the list performed?
● What are typical response rates for others who have used it?
● Can we have the list in a form that suits us, such as on disk or adhesive labels?

IDENTIFYING ITEMS TO INCLUDE IN A MAILSHOT

A mailshot can comprise nothing more than a simple postcard with a printed message. More usually, it is made up of an envelope containing one or more of the items shown:

- cover letter
- leaflet, brochure, or catalog
- promotional video
- customer newsletter
- product sample
- free gift
- money-off voucher
- order form
- coupon response device
- prepaid envelope

USING ENVELOPES

The envelope is a vital ingredient of your mailshot and has an important job to do. If you cannot encourage people to open the envelope, it is not worth spending money on what is inside. Some companies have found that envelopes resembling regular mail are most successful because customers tend to open a mailshot that looks like an ordinary letter. Other organizations have found that undisguised mailshots bring better results. Printed envelopes that urge the recipient to open the mailing, or that highlight the offer inside, are also effective. Innovative envelopes have novelty value and can attract attention, as can unusual sizes, shapes, textures, or color combinations, or unexpected materials such as foil, rubber, or plastic. Use gimmicky envelopes such as inflatables, or unusual fastenings such as Velcro. All can boost response rates, although they may be more expensive.

72 Make it easy for clients to update their details for your mailing list.

Unusual envelope and amusing free gift prompt recipient to read mailshot

ATTRACTING ATTENTION ▶
Regard your envelope as more than just a container for your mailshot. Consider using an unusual envelope which, although more expensive, can boost response rates.

CREATING THE PERFECT MAILSHOT

Maximize your marketing budget by developing the perfect mailing. You can achieve this by testing what works best, working with one variable at a time. Try out different mailing lists to find the best one, experiment with different offers to ascertain which is most attractive to customers, send mailings at different times to identify the best timing for a mailshot, and try out a variety of response devices to see which produces most replies. You can also use a technique known as split test mailing. If, for example, you want to test whether a price reduction produces a greater response, send half of your mailing list the standard offer and the other half the discounted offer. Then compare the take-up from each half.

73 Think about expanding your mailing list into a database.

▼ GAUGING COST
A standard method of accurately measuring the impact of a direct mail campaign is known as "cost per response," which tells you how much you are paying to elicit each response.

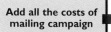

| Add all the costs of mailing campaign | Divide by number of responses | Ascertain cost per response |

74 Use bullet points to make benefits stand out from the main text.

75 Read your cover letter aloud. If it sounds stilted, rewrite it.

MEASURING CONVERSION

In addition to the "cost per response," there is another measurement that provides an insight into the effectiveness of a campaign. The "cost per conversion" tells you how much it costs to attract each sale. Divide the total cost of the mailing by the number of sales. At the outset, establish an allowable cost per conversion. Only you can decide what is acceptable. If an average customer spends $10,000 a year with you, $100 appears an acceptable investment to win such a customer. However, $100 is too much to pay if the annual transaction value per customer is only $35. If your allowable cost per conversion is $100, and you mail 10,000 packs (which cost $1 each), you will need to make 100 sales to break even.

Using the Internet

Everyone seems to want a presence in cyberspace, and more organizations are getting online daily. Make sure that you stay ahead of the competition by developing your own website, and learn how to use the internet as a powerful sales channel.

 76 Avoid hyphens in domain names; they complicate a web address.

 **77** Visit competitors' sites and collect useful ideas for your own.

78 Onscreen reading is harder on the eye, so keep text legible.

Developing a Website

Since your website may be the first point of contact for customers, it is very important that it reflects the right image. Templates enabling you to build your own website are available to download from the internet, but it takes an expert to design a well-executed site. Professional web designers know all the tricks. They can help ensure that your site pops up when potential customers use a search engine to hunt for you and link you to other sites. They can also advise on domain names, as well as securing and registering one for you, and they will, for a fee, maintain your site and keep it up to date on your behalf.

The Pros and Cons of Internet Selling

Attributes	Limitations
Conveys a massive amount of information.	Fraud presents problems for buyers and sellers.
Provides a gateway to new markets.	Buying online concerns some customers.
Enables instant feedback from customers.	Hacking and viruses are an ever-present threat.
The number of "hits," or visitors, attracted can be measured.	It is impossible to go to consumers; they must come to you.
Available 24 hours – the internet never sleeps.	Not everyone is online.

MAKING THE MOST OF YOUR WEBSITE

Consider carefully how you will use your site and have it constructed around your needs. Think about how the internet will fit into your overall marketing plan. It should be tackled not in isolation but as a component part of a much wider-ranging strategy. Your site can be used for:

● interactive publicity;

● customer support via email;

● maintaining relationships with existing customers and attracting new clients;

● generating interest in and building awareness of your product, service, or organization;

● conducting market research;

● selling products and services online;

● providing product information and current availability.

◀ VESTING CONTROL

Traditional publicity is relatively passive: organizations push it at consumers. The internet is a proactive medium: customers pull the information that they want.

ADVERTISING IN CYBERSPACE

Advertising on the internet continues to develop. It is inexpensive and measurable, interactive, sometimes fun, and can be viewed anytime. Use it to reach new markets locally, nationally, and globally. Make your website a promotional tool in its own right, so that it acts as an interactive brochure. Advertise on others' sites, perhaps with banner advertisements, which are the main advertising vehicle on the net, or animated or static ads, often found on search engine sites, which, if clicked on, lead viewers directly to your site. Sponsor other related sites that can provide a route to your own site. Web brokers will offer demographic information to help you decide where and how to advertise on the net, and they will also negotiate the space for you.

POINTS TO REMEMBER

● Your website should be designed to reflect your corporate image.

● A website should be easy and quick to navigate.

● Prospective clients may leave your site and visit those of competitors if your pages are elaborately designed and take a long time to download.

● It should be possible to return to the home page with one click.

● Including an email link will allow visitors to get in touch easily.

● Registering with directories may help publicize your site.

● A site needs maintaining to keep it fresh, current, and relevant.

CREATING A VIRTUAL STORE

E-commerce is a major growth area because it provides a fast, cost-efficient, "open all hours" way of selling. Setting up shop on the web is a very different undertaking from simply having a website. Once you begin to sell online, you are entering a new world, and internal restructuring will be needed. Set about establishing an order management system, comprising interactive order forms, order handling and tracking, a safe and secure payment environment, automated invoicing, and order fulfillment and delivery systems – orders may arrive from anywhere in the world. Some products do not lend themselves well to online selling (those that need to be touched or felt), while others are made for it (music or software, which can be downloaded directly from the net). Consider how an online storefront will affect your existing selling channels.

79 Register with net directories to ensure that your site is publicized.

▼ **ANALYZING WEBSITE USES**
A website can have numerous marketing applications. Use it to build and maintain customer relationships via email, for selling, promoting awareness of products or services to a wider market, giving up-to-date information, and so on.

80 Update the information on your site regularly.

81 Decide whether your products are suitable for selling online.

QUESTIONS TO ASK YOURSELF

Q Are our customers online?

Q Is our product or service suitable for online sales?

Q Do we want to limit our online presence to the publicizing of our venture?

Q Are our competitors online?

Q Do we have the skills to create and maintain our site?

Q Do we want to sell via the internet and could we handle the extra orders?

EMAILING CUSTOMERS

While poorly targeted direct mail is called junk mail, the email equivalent is known as "spam." Mass emailing (or spamming) to cold prospects is bad netiquette and will only result in damage to your reputation. However, email contact with customers and prospects can work to your advantage. Email provides an extremely cheap way to maintain a lasting relationship. Ask visitors to your website if they want to receive emailed updates, information, special offers, or details of new products; many will say yes. Ask current customers for their email details. Always keep an up-to-date emailing list and find legitimate excuses to get in contact. Remember to include a simple opt-out so that customers can ask to be removed from your emailing list if they wish.

REASSURING VIRTUAL CUSTOMERS

The internet is no longer new, yet there is still wariness about internet shopping. Scare stories about fraud and unfulfilled orders abound. Give customers confidence in your website. Explain how credit card payments can be made securely and safely. Create a customer charter or statement of rights to reassure people that it is safe to buy online from you. Explain clearly what your refund policy is. Publish your complaints procedure. Include an address, telephone and fax number, and a contact name, so that customers have other means of getting in touch if necessary.

82 Create a short domain name that is easy to spell and remember.

Customer is impressed that he is able to exchange goods bought on the internet at one of the supplier's retail outlets

◄ INSTILLING CONFIDENCE
Where possible, allow customers to use both your virtual store and traditional outlets, if you have them. If customers buy on the net, let them exchange goods through your retail stores.

DEVELOPING A STRATEGY

A strategy gives businesses a defined route to follow and a clear destination. Build a marketing strategy, and you will ensure that marketing is a long-term way of working, not a onetime activity.

THINKING STRATEGICALLY

When devising a marketing strategy, getting started can be the hardest part. Bring together a strong team to help plan your approach, and make sure that everyone understands the strategic elements that contribute to marketing success.

83 Allow plenty of time so that key decisions are not rushed.

84 Work on your marketing strategy when it is quiet to aid concentration.

GAINING FROM A STRATEGIC APPROACH

A marketing strategy provides organizations with a shared vision of the future. All too often, an organization will perform a marketing task, such as a direct mailshot, then sit back and see what happens. Or, as a knee-jerk reaction to falling sales or competitor activity, it might follow it up with a promotional offer, almost as if the organization is making up marketing as it goes along. A strategic approach will ensure that you maximize returns on your marketing spending and boost the profits of your organization.

STRATEGIC MANAGER	NON-STRATEGIC MANAGER
Has a clear picture of the future	Lives day to day without planning
Anticipates changes in the market	Reacts to changes in the market
Works toward clear, long-term goals	Has only short-term objectives

BUILDING A TEAM

Producing a marketing strategy from scratch can be daunting, especially if you are not a marketing specialist. Pull together a marketing strategy team from a range of departments to assist with drawing up future plans. Involve people whose function touches on marketing, and those whose job involves considerable customer contact. Before embarking on your marketing strategy, establish common ground by agreeing on definitions and purpose. Build team unity, perhaps by organizing a day out of the office at a pleasant venue to discuss shared marketing issues and concerns. Show that you recognize the contribution each team member can offer. Establish your authority as team leader by chairing meetings and overseeing follow-up activity.

▲ BEING AN EFFECTIVE MARKETING MANAGER

A successful marketing manager is strategic in outlook, ensuring maximum returns on marketing spending and boosting profits. A nonstrategic manager has no clear, long-term strategic objective in mind.

85 Choose team members for their range of skills.

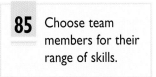

External consultant is able to offer impartial advice

USING A ▶ FACILITATOR

Consider bringing in an external facilitator or a marketing expert to work with the team and to keep you focused.

ANALYZING YOUR SITUATION

Planning your future marketing strategy is much more effective if you begin by examining the present. Study all aspects of your organization: your products and services, your customers, your market, and your competitors. Look closely at the marketing activity you currently undertake as well as the reasoning behind it. Ask yourself why you adopt certain working practices. Are there strong reasons for undertaking marketing activity in the way you do, or is it merely force of habit? What are your marketing successes? What about your failures? Examine your position in the marketplace and see how you compare with your competitors. Build up a realistic picture of your organization as it is today. Now you are ready to look to tomorrow.

PLANNING YOUR APPROACH

Work out how long you will need to develop the strategy, bearing in mind all the stages involved. Ensure that everyone on your team can dedicate the necessary time to the task. Map out a process for producing the strategy. This may comprise weekly team meetings, with individual tasking/follow-up work in between. Set a deadline for the completion of the strategy to keep the momentum going. Agree on dates in advance for all meetings and enter them into engagement calendars to ensure that there is little excuse for non-attendance. Keep notes of meetings and principal decisions and circulate these to team members.

CREATING A STRATEGY

Create your team

Review current situation

Set objectives

Plan action

Implement strategy

Review strategy

QUESTIONS TO ASK YOURSELF

Q Is there anyone else I should really have on the team?

Q Will we need to report to anyone higher up the ladder, such as the chief executive?

Q How long should I allow for the planning process?

Q Would it be helpful to engage an external marketing expert to help guide the planning process?

PERFORMING A SWOT ANALYSIS

The acronym SWOT stands for Strengths, Weaknesses, Opportunities, and Threats. Analysis of these four factors provides information on how to shape your marketing strategy. Devise objectives aimed at strengthening weak areas, exploiting strengths, seizing opportunities, and anticipating threats. To help your analysis, list your strengths, then ask the following questions:

- Do you use your strengths to full advantage? Could you do more to capitalize on them?
- Are there current or future opportunities you could exploit? Are new markets emerging or are there existing, untapped customer groups?
- What threats do your competitors pose? What threats exist in the wider marketplace?
- What lets you down? What are you not good at? What do your competitors do better?

86 Set a deadline for the completion of your strategy.

87 SWOT analyze competitors to see how you compare.

▼ **STEPPING STONES TO MARKETING SUCCESS**

All marketing strategies comprise three main stages: first, determine what you want to achieve; next, adopt the right approach or method to achieve that aim; finally, measure performance to gauge the level of success.

Aim → **Act** → **Assess**

INVOLVING ▶ COLLEAGUES

Ellie was in charge of sales for a small firm making sofa beds. Although not trained in marketing, she was also given overall responsibility for the company's marketing activity. She discovered the benefits of involving colleagues in major marketing initiatives.

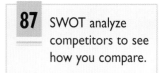

Without consulting her colleagues, Ellie decided to launch a website to attract new business. It was an enormous success, with 40 orders received on the first day. Unfortunately, these were from different parts of the country, which posed distribution problems (the company's orders had previously come from local retailers, making deliveries quick and simple). Given that the production department already had an order of 500 sofa beds

for a new hotel, they were unable to meet all the delivery dates, and the new customers were disappointed. This embarrassing situation made Ellie realize that she had to include members of the production and dispatch departments in the planning of any future promotional activity so that they could share important information about busy periods, existing commitments, and distribution problems with her.

SETTING OBJECTIVES

A strategy is a plan of action devised to meet certain objectives. Draw up your objectives carefully, because your entire marketing strategy will be structured around them, and ensure that they are measurable so that you can evaluate their success.

88 Take time to plan your marketing objectives carefully.

89 Set objectives that are challenging yet achievable.

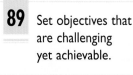

PLANNING OBJECTIVES

Analyze current position

Specify ideal and modify to incorporate reality

Define measurable short- and long-term objectives

Seek advice or views of colleagues

Modify and finalize objectives

TAKING STOCK

Objectives are goals that are drawn up to take your organization from its current position to where you would like it to be in the future. Short-term objectives can be staging posts on the way toward fulfilling long-term goals. Analyze your situation and then ask: "what if we do nothing?" Will products become out of date? Will your customers remain loyal to a company stuck in a time warp? Will your competitors grow more powerful? Spend time asking "what if?" to help you realize the effects of not keeping up with customer needs and competitors' activities. It can serve to spur action.

CREATING A VISION

Ask yourself where, in an ideal world, you would like your organization to be in five years' time. What position would you like to attain in the marketplace? Would you like to achieve significant growth in your customer base and profitability? Would you like to be the brand leader? Paint a picture of the perfect scenario. Now bring a little reality to bear. Think about likely economic, legal, technological, social, and political changes. Will they pose opportunities or threats? Modify the ideal situation to take account of the realities of the market. What is achievable if you work really hard at it? Keep a record of your ideas.

DEVISING OBJECTIVES

The framework for your objectives has already been created in your vision of the future. Now take each of your goals for the future and translate it into an objective. Remember that an objective simply states what you want to achieve, not how you will achieve it. Each one should have both a quantity and a timeframe. These will help you to tighten the focus of your objective and to measure success. Some objectives will be achievable in the near future: these are your short-term goals. Others will be longer term. Organize objectives into short- and long-term so that you can manage the workload that goes with turning goals into reality. Phrase them so that they are clear and unambiguous.

▼ MAKING OBJECTIVES MEASURABLE

Underneath your vision, list your objectives, then quantify each one and set out a date or timescale within which the objective will be achieved. This enables you to evaluate progress and measure success far more effectively.

Future vision

To be the premier player in our field

Objectives	Quantity	Timeframe
To increase our customer base	By 25 percent	Within 12 months
To widen our product range	With the introduction of two new lines	By the end of January
To raise our customer profile	So that consumer awareness of the organization and products is boosted by 20 percent	Nine months into the profile-raising campaign

90 Set at least one objective that can be achieved imminently.

91 Discuss objectives with colleagues to ensure their support.

GAINING AGREEMENT

Once you have devised a set of objectives around which to build your marketing strategy, seek agreement for them from across the organization. Marketing is a discipline that cuts through many departmental boundaries. Marketing activity will have a knock-on effect in various parts of the operation so, for it to be effective, you will need the support of colleagues. Ensure they understand the need for these objectives and the impact they may have on their work. Listen to any objections they may have and assess their validity. It is better to spend time discussing objectives at this stage, so that they can be modified where necessary before you invest considerable effort in devising ways of achieving your goals.

ACHIEVING YOUR GOALS

Having established your objectives, now work out how you are going to attain your ultimate goal. Investigate constraints, such as time and money, and then create a timetable of activity to give you a working marketing plan.

92 Encourage full participation at brainstorming sessions.

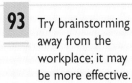

93 Try brainstorming away from the workplace; it may be more effective.

DEVISING SOLUTIONS ▼

Discuss each suggestion put forward during a brainstorming session. If an idea seems unworkable at first, encourage the team to think of innovative solutions rather than to discard it without consideration.

BRAINSTORMING IDEAS

Coming up with ideas for achieving your objectives is a creative process. The best technique for freeing creativity is brainstorming. Display an objective on an overhead, screen, or flipchart. Next, ask your strategy team to suggest ideas for helping achieve that objective. Write all ideas on a flipchart. Do not comment on, assess, discuss, or evaluate ideas at this stage. Simply record all suggestions. Aim to attract as many ideas as possible and encourage all group members to participate.

Team member suggests sending written product briefing to all customers each month

Colleague questions whether idea would be affordable in terms of time and money

Team member suggests email briefing would be both easy and cheap

Manager agrees that modified idea is good and agrees to implement it

SETTING BUDGETS

Look at your marketing ideas and work out the cost of each. Remember that marketing involves meeting customer need at a profit. To be justified, marketing activity should have a positive impact on the balance sheet. Examine not only the cost but also the benefit. An advertising campaign may cost a lot of money, but if it reaps profits amounting to several times its cost, it is cheap. Avoid setting an overall marketing budget to start with. Instead, work out costs and outcomes, decide what is justified, then calculate the budget.

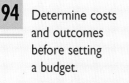

94 Determine costs and outcomes before setting a budget.

▼ **SETTING OUT A PLAN**
Some marketing ideas will require little time or money to implement. Others will be costly and/or complicated. List your ideas and give them a high, medium, or low priority. Then assign start and completion dates. Consider implementing low priority ideas immediately if they are quick, cheap, and easy.

POINTS TO REMEMBER

● The costs of not undertaking certain marketing activities, both in missed opportunities and the effect on your reputation, should be taken into consideration.

● The activities on your marketing timetable should be manageable and workable.

TIMETABLING ACTIVITIES

Prioritize activities and then organize it into a logical order. Put a date alongside each activity. When assigning dates, consider the importance of timing. Some ideas are best undertaken when there is an obvious marketing link. For example, if you manufacture pumpkin pies, aim to tie in your promotion with a significant or high profile event, such as Thanksgiving Day. When timetabling, bear in mind the impact that your marketing activities will have on internal resources. Avoid time-intensive activities during periods of high staff absence, such as during the summer vacation period. Remember that this timetable is your working marketing plan.

MARKETING PLAN

ACTIVITY	PRIORITY	START DATE	COMPLETION DATE
Organize lunch for top ten customers	Medium		by end February
Produce new brochure	High	mid-January	end March
Update mailing list ready for new brochure	High		end March
Mail new brochure	High	early April	

EFFECTING THE STRATEGY

Producing a marketing strategy is a means to an end; results will come from implementing it. Assign tasks to staff, provide any support they need, then review progress, measure performance, and periodically revise objectives.

95 Ask for regular progress reports, specifying which facts you need.

96 Make sure that staff inform you of implementation delays and difficulties.

ASSIGNING ACTIVITIES

Some organizations invest considerable effort in developing a strategy, but enthusiasm and energy wane when it comes to implementation. Ensure that your marketing strategy is put into action, not left to gather dust on a shelf. Assign each task or activity due for implementation within the next 12 months to a named person. Check that anyone given responsibility for an activity has the time, knowledge, expertise, budget, and authority to complete the task. Give clear instructions on what is expected and by when. If necessary, ask for regular progress reports, so that you are assured everything is running according to plan.

◀ **REVIEWING PROGRESS**

The general marketing forum might be open to a large number of staff. In addition to this you will need a smaller review group. This might comprise the original marketing strategy team. Meet at least quarterly, possibly more often. The purpose of this group is to compare progress against planned activity.

ACTIONING THE PLAN

Make sure you allow staff to get on with their marketing tasks, but, equally, make sure you do not neglect them. Create a forum for those involved in the creation and implementation of the strategy so that problems and difficulties can be discussed. Work together to devise solutions. Build a supportive atmosphere, rewarding those who are staying on course and encouraging those who are not. Although staff may be involved in implementing only a small part of the strategy, an inclusive forum will enable them to see the bigger picture. Use the forum to receive and discuss progress reports. By sharing these with staff, you will help them to see the benefits of the marketing activity and strengthen their commitment to implementing a successful strategy.

QUESTIONS TO ASK YOURSELF

Q Have profits increased since the strategy was implemented?

Q Have we seen an increase in our customer base?

Q Have we attracted a greater number of orders, or larger individual orders?

Q Has the number of product/ service enquiries risen?

Q Has awareness of our organization and its products or services increased?

▼ REVISING OBJECTIVES

The world is not static. Things within your organization or within your market are likely to change over time. If they do, you might need to redefine your objectives. Review objectives semiannually or annually to check that you are still on track.

97 After delegating a task, try to avoid interfering unless there is a risk that objectives will not be met.

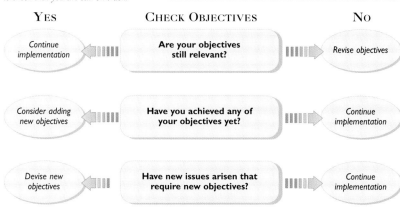

YES	CHECK OBJECTIVES	NO
Continue implementation	Are your objectives still relevant?	Revise objectives
Consider adding new objectives	Have you achieved any of your objectives yet?	Continue implementation
Devise new objectives	Have new issues arisen that require new objectives?	Continue implementation

GAINING SUPPORT

Marketing has a vital role to play in every organization, but its contribution is not always recognized. As part of your strategy, build support within the workplace. Break down departmental barriers and help create a marketing organization.

98 Explain how marketing can support colleagues in their work.

99 Make colleagues aware of marketing successes.

100 Cultivate the support of all your colleagues.

WINNING ALLIES

Marketing managers often complain that their departments are always blamed when things go wrong and are never credited when they go well. It can be difficult for staff on the frontline of the business to see the relevance of marketing. Win the support, understanding, commitment, and collaboration of your nonmarketing colleagues, including the chairperson and chief executive. Tell them of your organization's marketing successes. Show them what effective marketing can achieve, and use hard data to demonstrate its benefits.

BECOMING A MARKETING ORGANIZATION

If staff across the organization can see the relevance and benefits of marketing, their cooperation will follow naturally. They may offer sales leads, provide constructive feedback on marketing materials, or come up with workable ideas for improving customer service. Involve all staff in marketing activities. Ask for ideas and show that you value their contribution. In addition to telling them about your work, become acquainted with their work, too.

▼ SHARING SUCCESSES
Explain to colleagues how marketing techniques can be used to support them in their work. Involve relevant staff from other departments in marketing planning. Give them a stake in its success.

SHARING INFORMATION

Keep colleagues informed of any marketing activity. Staff sometimes grumble that they are the last people to hear about what the marketing department is doing; the first they may know about a new ad is when customers or friends tell them. When this happens, staff feel stupid, embarrassed, or ill-informed. Use memos and e-mails to brief colleagues. Let them feel that they have insider knowledge. Tell staff the day before a new press ad appears or a new radio ad is broadcast. Tip them off that a direct mail campaign is about to get underway. Obviously you will not wish to publicize commercially sensitive information, but there is no harm in keeping staff up to date and involved.

▲ SUPPORTING OTHER DEPARTMENTS
Find out what colleagues in different departments do from day to day and see if your marketing skills can help them provide a better service to customers.

POINTS TO REMEMBER

- Cross-organization support is required for effective marketing.
- The marketing department cannot operate in a vacuum.
- Colleagues should not be given an opportunity to question your value and contribution.

101 Be prepared to justify your existence in a positive way.

HANDLING SKEPTICISM

It is not unusual for employees to criticize other departments within their organization, and marketing often attracts more than its fair share of adverse comment. If people outside of the marketing department are heard complaining that "we do not know what marketing finds to do all day," or "marketing does not understand the realities of our work," you are working in a compartmentalized organization. If this is the case, do all that you can to cultivate the support and respect of colleagues in other departments. In a true marketing organization, all members of staff are able to see the direct benefit of marketing and are fully aware of how the marketing team contributes to its overall success.

ASSESSING YOUR MARKETING ABILITY

A good understanding of basic marketing theory, combined with experience of techniques, will ensure your ability to implement an effective marketing program. This questionnaire will test your approach to marketing. Answer the questions as honestly as you can. If your answer is "never", mark Option 1, and so on. Add your scores together, and refer to the Analysis at the end of the questionnaire.

OPTIONS

1 Never

2 Occasionally

3 Frequently

4 Always

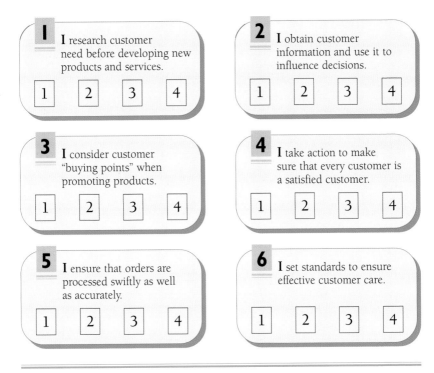

1 I research customer need before developing new products and services.

| 1 | 2 | 3 | 4 |

2 I obtain customer information and use it to influence decisions.

| 1 | 2 | 3 | 4 |

3 I consider customer "buying points" when promoting products.

| 1 | 2 | 3 | 4 |

4 I take action to make sure that every customer is a satisfied customer.

| 1 | 2 | 3 | 4 |

5 I ensure that orders are processed swiftly as well as accurately.

| 1 | 2 | 3 | 4 |

6 I set standards to ensure effective customer care.

| 1 | 2 | 3 | 4 |

7 I measure performance against the standards of customer care.

1 | 2 | 3 | 4

8 I take the complaints of customers very seriously.

1 | 2 | 3 | 4

9 I monitor the number of customer complaints that we receive.

1 | 2 | 3 | 4

10 I try to see if there is anything I can learn from a customer's complaint.

1 | 2 | 3 | 4

11 I find reasons to keep in touch with customers.

1 | 2 | 3 | 4

12 I try to turn onetime customers into regular ones.

1 | 2 | 3 | 4

13 I keep a record of key customer contact.

1 | 2 | 3 | 4

14 I ask customers whether they will recommend us.

1 | 2 | 3 | 4

15 I show customers that their business is valued.

1 | 2 | 3 | 4

16 I try to find out why we have lost a customer.

1 | 2 | 3 | 4

17 I attempt to win back lost customers.

1 2 3 4

18 I am on the lookout for new customers.

1 2 3 4

19 I try to nurture customer loyalty.

1 2 3 4

20 I seek customer comment and feedback.

1 2 3 4

21 I listen to what customers say.

1 2 3 4

22 I pay attention to the little details that make all the difference.

1 2 3 4

23 I try to add value to our products and services.

1 2 3 4

24 I emphasize benefits, not features.

1 2 3 4

25 I use public relations techniques to boost marketing effectiveness.

1 2 3 4

26 I draw up a pricing strategy for every new product marketed.

1 2 3 4

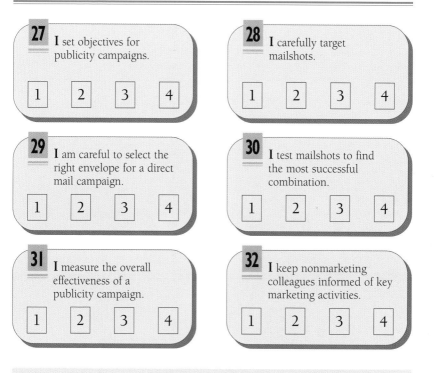

27 I set objectives for publicity campaigns.

| 1 | 2 | 3 | 4 |

28 I carefully target mailshots.

| 1 | 2 | 3 | 4 |

29 I am careful to select the right envelope for a direct mail campaign.

| 1 | 2 | 3 | 4 |

30 I test mailshots to find the most successful combination.

| 1 | 2 | 3 | 4 |

31 I measure the overall effectiveness of a publicity campaign.

| 1 | 2 | 3 | 4 |

32 I keep nonmarketing colleagues informed of key marketing activities.

| 1 | 2 | 3 | 4 |

ANALYSIS

Now that you have completed the self-assessment, add up your total score and check your performance. Whatever level of success you have achieved, there is always room for improvement. Identify your weakest areas, then refer to the relevant sections of this book, where you will find practical advice and tips to help you establish and hone your marketing skills.
32–64: You need to take a more organized, planned, methodical, and measured approach to improve your effectiveness.
65–95: Some of your marketing activity is a success, but you need to develop your skills to become wholly effective.
96–128: You have adopted a thoroughly professional, strategic approach to marketing and are running successful marketing campaigns. Keep up the good work to stay ahead of the competition.

INDEX

ACKNOWLEDGMENTS

AUTHOR'S ACKNOWLEDGMENTS

I would like to thank everyone who helped on this book including my
brother Jez Ali for his support and assistance.

PUBLISHER'S ACKNOWLEDGMENTS

Dorling Kindersley would like to thank the following for their help and
participation in producing this book:

Photographer Matthew Ward.
Photographic assistance Silvia Bucher.

Models Tracey Allanson, Phil Argent, Jeanie Fraser, Mark Fraser, Aziz Khan,
Kaz Takabatake, Dominica Warburton.

Make-up Evelynne.

Picture research Anna Grapes, Andrea Stadler.
Picture library assistance Melanie Simmonds.

Indexer Hilary Bird.

PICTURE CREDITS

Key: *a* above, *b* bottom, *c* center, *l* left, *r* right, *t* top
Ace Photo Agency: 14*bl*; **Corbis UK Ltd:** 33*br*; **Pictor International:** 4-5, 11*bl*, 65*tr*;
Tony Stone Images: Alan Thornton 42*cb*; **Superstock Ltd.:** 39*bl*, 52*cr*;
Telegraph Colour Library: 62*bl*; **UPS:** 32*bl*.

AUTHOR'S BIOGRAPHY

Moi Ali has worked in marketing for over 15 years and runs her own public relations and
marketing company, specializing in clients with limited budgets – in particular small
businesses and charities. She is a regular contributor to marketing and PR journals and
is the author of a number of books.